PARAKEETS

Katie John

Grolier
an imprint of

www.scholastic.com/librarypublishing

Published 2009 by Grolier
An Imprint of Scholastic Library Publishing
Old Sherman Turnpike
Danbury, Connecticut 06816

For The Brown Reference Group plc
Project Editor: Jolyon Goddard
Picture Researchers: Clare Newman, Sophie Mortimer
Designer: Sarah Williams
Managing Editor: Tim Harris

Volume ISBN-13: 978-0-7172-8047-6
Volume ISBN-10: 0-7172-8047-0

Library of Congress Cataloging-in-Publication Data

Nature's children. Set 5.
p. cm.
Includes index.
ISBN-13: 978-0-7172-8084-1
ISBN-10: 0-7172-8084-5 (set)
1. Animals--Encyclopedias, Juvenile. I. Grolier Educational (Firm)
QL49.N386 2009
590.3--dc22
2008014674

Printed and bound in China

PICTURE CREDITS

Front Cover: **Shutterstock**: Gary Unwin.

Back Cover: **Shutterstock**: Peter Blottman, Pixelman, Gina Smith, YYS.

Alamy: Juniors Bildarchiv 17, 29, 33, 45, Petra Wegner 37, Maximilian Weinzierl 38; **Corbis**: Jim Craigmyle 46, Blaine Harrington III 22; **FLPA**: Tony Hamblin 21, David Hosking 14; **NaturePL**: Owen Newman 10, 12, Reinhard/ARCO 34, 42, Kim Taylor 4, Wegner/ARCO 30; **Photolibrary.com**: 6, 26–27; **Shutterstock**: Peter Blottman 2–3, Joanne Harris and Daniel Bubnich 5, 41, Gary Unwin 18; **Still Pictures**: Sailer/Schnizler 9.

Contents

FACT FILE: Parakeets

Class	Birds (Aves)
Order	Parrotlike birds (Psittaciformes)
Family	Parrots (Psittacidae)
Genus	*Melopsittacus*
Species	Parakeet or budgerigar (*Melopsittacus undulatus*)
World distribution	Found naturally in Australia, but kept in captivity all over the world
Habitat	Tropical and subtropical forests and scrublands
Distinctive physical characteristics	Small, hooked beak; each foot has four toes—two pointing forward and two backward; attractive, colorful feathers
Habits	Sociable and vocal; survive well in captivity; can be taught to "speak" a few words
Diet	Seeds; also leafy plants, vegetables, and fruit

Introduction

Humans have always admired birds for their beautiful **plumage** and amazing voices. Many types of birds, from dazzling parrots to sweet-voiced nightingales, were prized. Today, millions of birds are specially bred as pets.

Perhaps the world's favorite birds are parakeets, also known as budgies. Parakeets originated in Australia. They were first tamed in the mid-1800s. They were sent all over the world. Attractive and friendly, these little birds make ideal companions for anyone, young or old.

After cats and dogs, birds are the most popular kind of pet in the United States.

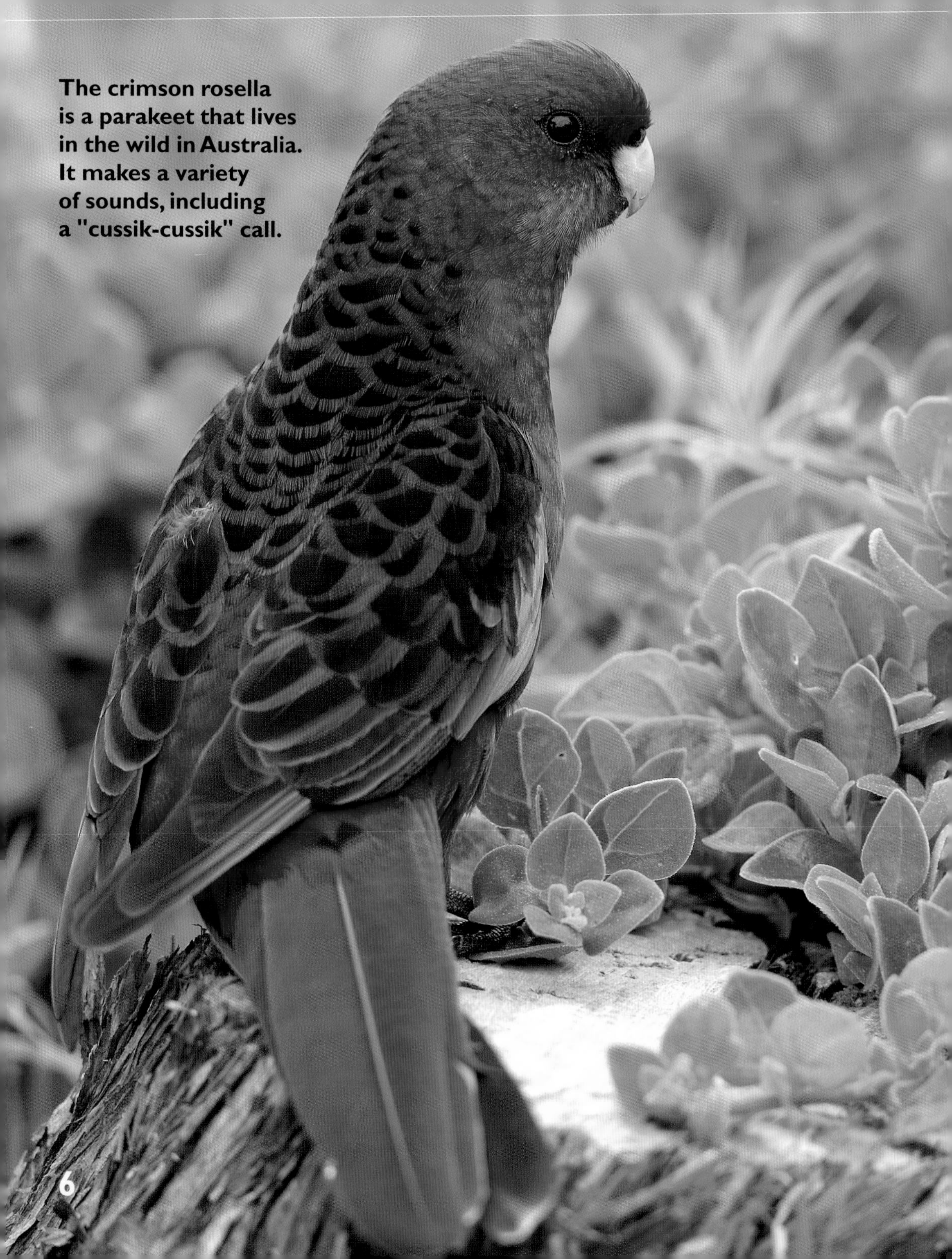

The crimson rosella is a parakeet that lives in the wild in Australia. It makes a variety of sounds, including a "cussik-cussik" call.

What's in a Name?

The name "parakeet" is used in most places to mean any kind of small parrot with a long, tapering tail. The birds that most North Americans call "parakeets" are known to bird experts and others as "budgerigars" or "budgies." This name comes from *gidjirrigaa*, a word used by the Kamilaroi people of southeast Australia. It is thought to mean "good cockatoo." Some people have even suggested that the name means "good eating"—sadly for the birds!

Other kinds of parakeets are often kept as pets or in nature parks. These include ringnecked parakeets, which come from central Africa and southern Asia. Monk parakeets—also known as Quaker parrots—come from South America. Rosellas, from Australia, are another popular type of parakeet. These birds are all bigger than budgies and look much more like parrots.

Family Features

Parakeets belong to the parrot family. They are among the smallest members of this group. Wild parakeets, or budgerigars, are about 7 inches (18 cm) long including the tail, and they weigh about 1 ounce (30 g). Tame ones are slightly bigger. "English budgies," which are bred for showing in competitions, are the largest, plumpest kind, weighing about 2 ounces (60 g).

Like other types of parrots, parakeets have a strong, hooked beak for opening nuts and seeds. Parakeets' feet have four toes each, and each toe ends in a nail-like claw. On each foot, two of the toes point forward and two point backward. These two pairs can be moved toward each other. This allows the birds to grip branches and climb around in treetops. Their narrow, pointed wings make them very fast, agile fliers that can easily escape from **predators**. Parakeets are very intelligent birds. They have strong social bonds with their family and the other members of their **flock**.

The parrot family contains more than 350 species of birds. Included in this family are macaws, lories, lovebirds, cockatoos, cockatiels, and budgerigars, such as this pair.

The green plumage of wild budgies helps them blend into the leaves of eucalyptus trees. That way predators cannot see them.

In the Wild

In Australia, flocks of parakeets still exist in the wild. They live in the woodlands and scrublands of this vast, dry country, often close to water. The birds make their nests in hollows in tree trunks or hollowed-out rotten logs. They eat seeds from grasses and leaves from trees. Certain types of eucalyptus trees are especially important for parakeets. Their leaves provide a necessary source of nutrients. In addition, the oil from the leaves has medicinal properties that help keep the birds free of disease. Even tame birds enjoy chewing eucalyptus branches.

Parakeets also spend a lot of their time in flight. They travel to new feeding grounds or fly away from predators such as hawks. They come together in tight formations, speeding and wheeling through the air in breathtaking **aerobatic** displays. Their long, slim wings and small, streamlined body are just right for this kind of life.

Australian Nomads

Wild budgerigars are **nomadic**. That means they travel great distances over the dry interior of Australia in search of food and water. They can travel up to 300 miles (480 km) in a day. Once the food and water in an area have become scarce, they take to the skies again to look for new feeding grounds. They often head to places that have just had rain or thunderstorms. In these places, they know they will find the nutritious grasses that grow for just a few hours or days after a heavy rainfall.

The birds seem to know or sense when rain has fallen, even from far away. They take off, circling high in the air, and then head straight for that place.

When food is very scarce, several flocks of wild budgerigars might join together.

Budgerigars have excellent eyesight. This group is on the lookout for fresh food.

Flocking Together

Being part of a flock is very important to parakeets. By sticking together, they can find food and avoid predators more easily. Having company also keeps the birds happy and healthy. They like to have someone else to "talk to" or play with. In addition, flock members help teach the youngest birds important lessons for life, such as what to eat and how to get along with others.

The birds communicate by using their voices. They call to one another when they wake up, before they go to sleep, and while they are flying, to make sure nobody is missing. They shriek in alarm to warn the others of danger, or to drive intruders away from their nest. And they continually chatter to their **mate**, chicks, or young, and friends. Tame parakeets are the same. They see the humans who look after them as part of their "flock."

Amazing Colors

Modern parakeets look very different from their ancestors. Wild Australian budgerigars always have green plumage, with yellow head feathers and black, wavy patterns of feathers on the back of their head and wings. They have a dark blue or purple patch on each cheek, and black spots around the throat.

Today, parakeets exist in more than 100 colors and patterns. They are often green. But they can be sky-blue, dark blue, white, gray, yellow, and even mauve. There are also mixtures such as blue with a yellow head or mauve with a white head.

Here's something amazing. Parakeets can glow in the dark! The feathers on their head are **fluorescent**, and this effect can be seen under ultraviolet light—a form of sunlight that is invisible to us, but can be seen by the birds. The parakeets use their fluorescent feathers in **courtship displays**, to attract a mate.

Blue budgerigars were sought after by bird owners and were sold for very high prices.

The male of this courting pair of budgies is perched on the left. He has a blue cere at the top of his beak.

Who's Who?

It is usually easy to tell male and female parakeets apart, by looking at the **cere** (SIR). That's the fleshy part just above the bird's beak, where its nostrils are. In adult male birds, the cere is blue. In females it is brown or beige. Younger females sometimes also have thin rings around the nostrils. In young birds and **albinos**—birds that are white all over with pink eyes—the cere is pink.

Young birds less than four months old usually have black lines, or bars, over the whole of their head, not just at the back. For this reason, they are sometimes called "barheads." They also have totally dark eyes, while adults usually have light gray **irises**.

Budgie Babies

Wild budgerigars start to **breed** as soon as they are adults. However, they will only breed when their living conditions will allow them to support chicks. The weather has to be just right—not too hot or cold. Often, rainfall makes them ready to breed, because it means good supplies of water and nutritious food.

Pairs of domestic parakeets are ready to breed when they are one year old. They will need a special nest box. Females lay a **clutch** of three to six eggs, laying one every couple of days. The eggs hatch 18 to 20 days later. The chicks' eyes open at about 10 days old, and their feathers start appearing at 15 days. They **fledge** and take their first flight at about five weeks of age. In the first couple of weeks, the chicks' mother takes care of them while the father finds food. Later, both parents care for them until they can feed themselves.

These four-day-old chicks are helpless. They wait for food and huddle around an unhatched egg.

Budgies and other types of parakeets are popular worldwide. This parakeet from Panama is tame enough to perch on a person's hand.

Owning Birds

You might want a parakeet as a pet to play with or to talk to you. But, you need to think about what you can give to your bird. First, you need to set aside enough time to care for your bird every day. Second, parakeets have to have company. It is possible to keep one bird by itself, and it will form a bond with its owner. But no person can be there all the time, and a lonely bird can become very unhappy. It is better to get at least two birds, so they can keep one another company. You also need to remember that parakeets can live from 10 to 15 years—so they are a long-term commitment. If you are prepared to give your birds what they need, you will be rewarded with loving, delightful pets.

Making a Home

For parakeets, bigger homes are better. Their cage needs to be longer than it is high, so the birds can fly around. A good-sized cage for two birds is 40 inches (1 m) long, 20 inches (0.5 m) deep, and 32 inches (0.8 m) high. That will allow plenty of room for flying, and also for "furniture" such as perches. If you plan to keep a lot of birds, you will need a much bigger enclosure, called an **aviary**.

The birdcage should have horizontal bars, spaced about half an inch (1 cm) apart. That width allows the birds to climb around the cage—including upside down. That distance between the bars is too narrow for their head, so they will not get it stuck! Check that the bars are made out of **nontoxic** metal, such as stainless steel. The cage will also need a solid base for the birds to walk on. Many birdcages are fitted with a removable plastic tray, which makes cleaning up easier.

A Place to Perch

Your parakeets' cage will need two or three perches for the birds to sit on. These should be made of wood, not plastic, and be different widths, so the birds' feet do not become sore and cramped in one position all the time. Set the perches at different levels, including one fairly high up. You can also use tree branches as natural perches, as long as you choose wood that is safe for birds, such as apple or maple. Make sure the branches have not been sprayed with chemicals, and wash and dry them before adding them to the cage.

You will need two food cups. One is for dry foods, such as seeds, and the other is for moist foods, such as leaves. Fit these cups to the side of the cage, just beside the perches. The birds will also need a cup or feeding bottle for water.

Like their wild relatives, pet budgerigars enjoy the company of other budgies.

Prime Locations

As part of the family, parakeets will want to be where the action is. The best place for their cage is in a room where people spend a lot of time, such as a family room. Parakeets should be let out to fly whenever possible. Before letting them out of the cage, make sure the room has no dangerous items, such as gas fires, ceiling fans, or copper pipes. Never put a cage in a kitchen, because food and cooking pots give off fumes that can be dangerous to birds.

Birds do not like having their home moved around, so you need to choose a good spot right from the start. Find a place where the birds will get plenty of light. Never put a cage close to a door or window, because your birds could get chilled by drafts or overheated by sunlight. Never use household cleaners, sprays, or candles around birds, or let people smoke tobacco near them.

Make sure all windows and doors are closed before letting pet parakeets out of their cage.

Budgies should stay with their parents until they are at least four months old. These two-week-old chicks are much too young to be given new homes as pets.

Choosing Birds

To have the greatest chance of forming close bonds with your parakeets, it is best to get them while they are still young. A good age is about four months, when the birds are young adults and have had some handling, but are still young enough to learn new things and adapt to a new home. It is best to get two males or two females, and buy them at the same time so they are together from the start. Males are thought to be easier to handle and train.

Look for birds that are active and curious, and seem friendly. Check that they are healthy. Their feathers should be sleek, the eyes bright and clear, and the nostrils and **vent** clean. Avoid birds with a red cere or eyes, those with ruffled or dirty feathers, or any that sit silently on the floor of the cage.

Food and Drink

Wild budgerigars are mostly vegetarian. Their main food is grass seeds, but they also eat leaves and a few grubs or insects. Tame birds should have a similar diet. Pet stores sell seed mixes for parakeets, but they need fresh food, too. Leafy plants that humans eat, such as lettuce and spinach—but not cabbage—parsley, or even dandelion leaves, are good choices. Parakeets may also enjoy grated carrot or a slice of apple wedged in the bars of the cage. Wash these foods first. Do not offer your pet bird avocado or chocolate because they are poisonous to parakeets.

Your parakeets will also need extra nutrients. They can get these by pecking at a **cuttlebone**, which will help keep them healthy. Chewing on the bone also trims their beak. Parakeets only eat the soft insides of seeds. They do not need to swallow grit to help crush their food as many other birds do.

A bird's beak is made of keratin—a tough substance that also makes up fingernails. Like a fingernail, the beak never stops growing. Pecking at a cuttlebone helps a budgie keep its beak just the right length.

Millet sprays make a perch and are also a tasty treat for budgies.

Keeping Clean

It is very important to clean your parakeets' cage, food cups, and water bottles regularly. This will keep your birds healthy and comfortable. Every day, give your parakeets fresh food and water, and wash the cups and bottles. Do not leave vegetables or fruit in the cage for more than an hour, otherwise they will start to spoil.

The easiest way to keep the cage clean is to line the bottom with newspaper. But, do not use newspaper with colored ink, because that is poisonous to the birds. Change the paper every day. Once a week, wash the whole cage, including the bottom and the perches, with hot water and a disinfectant that is safe for birds. You will need to take your birds out and have someone watch them while you are cleaning the cage. Rinse everything thoroughly, and make sure it is dry before putting the birds back.

A Daily Routine

All birds, including parakeets, like to have a regular schedule. In the wild, they wake up at sunrise, sleep for a while at midday, and go to bed at sunset. It is best to "put your birds to bed" in the middle of the evening, so they get 10 to 12 hours' rest. To make sure they have a peaceful night, cover the cage with a blanket. Uncover the cage at the same time each morning. Birds like to get food and water at about the same time each day.

Also, take a few minutes each day to check on your parakeets. Watch out for any changes in the way they look or behave. Look in their seed bowl and blow across the top of it. That makes empty **husks** fall out so the birds can find more seeds to eat.

During sleep, a budgie closes its eyes and rests its head on its back.

Budgies shed and replace their feathers as they become worn and lose their ability to keep the bird warm or streamlined for flight.

Beauty Tips

Bathing helps parakeets keep their feathers and skin healthy. Wild budgerigars often splash in shallow water or rub themselves in wet leaves after it has rained. You can give a pet bird a bath by putting a shallow dish of water in the cage, or by putting in a bowl of clean, wet lettuce or eucalyptus leaves. It is best to let the birds bathe in the morning, so they have plenty of time to dry off. Remove the bath or leaves as soon as they have finished.

Parakeets also **preen** themselves to keep their feathers in good condition. Preening also helps remove loose feathers when the birds are **molting**. Budgies often carry out preening sessions all at the same time, and even groom one another on hard-to-reach places, such as their head. That's what friends are for!

Basic Lessons

A pet bird can be trained to do certain things, such as stepping from a perch onto your finger. The most important part of training a bird is to get it used to being held. Allow about 15 minutes each day. First, just put your hand in the cage, and talk softly. It can help to offer a treat, such as millet seeds. When the bird is happy with that, pick up one of the perches in the cage and hold it close to the bird's feet. Once the bird has accepted your hand with the perch, the next step is to press your index finger gently on the underside of the bird's lower body, while saying "UP." The bird should learn to step up onto your finger. Let him or her sit there for a few minutes, then slowly move your finger toward a perch, and say "DOWN" as the bird steps off. Use the same words every time. Soon, the bird will be comfortable perched on your finger or sitting in your hand.

A bird owner should always wash his or her hands after handling a bird. Pet birds can pass on bugs to humans.

To keep a single bird happy, toys such as a plastic rocking budgie can provide fun and distraction.

Fun and Games

Play time is important for keeping your parakeets entertained. They will probably be most active in the mornings and afternoons. As well as playing with one another or you, parakeets love toys, especially toys that they can climb on, chew, or rip to pieces. "Chew toys" made of nontoxic wood are good for parakeets, because the wood stops their beak from becoming too long. Female birds tend to chew more than males. That's because in the wild female parakeets chew wood to make nesting holes and a soft floor covering inside them.

An ideal basic toy is the center from a roll of toilet paper, which the birds can rip up. You can also buy special toys such as swings and balls. Make sure such toys have no parts that could become entangled with your birds or pieces that they could chew off and swallow. Offer two or three toys at a time. Keep a selection so the birds do not get bored. Wash the toys regularly.

Learning to Talk

Most parakeets will chirp or chatter when they hear people's voices. They will also mimic, or copy, certain sounds, such as the ring of a telephone. However, if you want to teach a bird to say words, it is best to get a young male and keep him by himself. This lifestyle is unnatural for parakeets, so you will have to give the bird a lot of attention to make up for it. Teach just one or two words at a time, and repeat several times each day.

Even if your birds never learn to speak, they will enjoy hearing familiar words, such as "hello," "good bird," and their name. It is just as important for you to learn bird language, too! Watch them to see which sounds and body movements they make to show different moods and feelings. Examples include gentle beak-grinding when they are happy, or flattening the feathers and screeching when they are scared or angry.

Pet budgies can learn to say many human words. One budgie even learned more than 1,700 words in its lifetime.

If you're unsure about your pet bird's health, take it to your vet. The vet will be able to quickly see any signs of disease.

Health Care

The best way to keep parakeets healthy is to get to know them as individuals. That way, you can easily see any changes in their condition. Parakeets hide signs of sickness for as long as possible. This is because in the wild, sick birds are rejected by the flock or eaten by predators. If you can notice warning signs, you can deal with problems before they become too bad.

A sick bird may be quieter and less active than usual. He or she may sit fluffed up at the bottom of the cage. The bird might eat less than usual. The **droppings** may be runny, or an unusual color, and may dirty the feathers around the vent. Other warning signs include a discharge from the bird's nostrils, wheezing, and tail-bobbing as the bird struggles to breathe. If you see any of these signs, or if you just suspect that something is wrong, take your bird to a veterinarian—a doctor for animals.

In-flight Safety

Parakeets have wings and like to use them! Therefore, you should allow them to fly around your home from time to time. Before you let them out for flying practice, check that the room will be safe for them. Remove any poisonous potted plants or flowers in vases, such as asparagus ferns, poinsettia, tomato plants, and daffodils. Check that there are no poisonous kinds of wood, such as oak or yew, in the room, and no copper or brass ornaments. Chewing or pecking at any of those could make a parakeet very ill. Close any possible escape routes, such as doors and windows. It is also a good idea to close curtains and cover mirrors, so the birds will not crash into the glass.

Stay with your birds whenever they are flying free, and keep watch so you do not sit or step on them. Make sure they do not chew electrical cords, or get too close to breakable objects that could hurt them. Apart from that, enjoy watching your birds have fun!

Words to Know

Aerobatic Very skilled at moving in the air during flight.

Albinos Animals with no pigment in their skin. Albinos have white feathers or hair and pink eyes.

Aviary A big enclosure, usually built outdoors, where birds can fly freely.

Breed To produce babies or—in the case of birds—chicks.

Cere A fleshy place on a bird's head just above the beak.

Clutch A group of eggs.

Courtship displays Behaviors designed to attract a mate, usually performed by males. In parakeets, they include bobbing the head and giving food to the mate.

Cuttlebone The skeleton of a cuttlefish. Cuttlebones are a source of calcium, which keeps a parakeet's bones, heart, muscles, and nerves healthy.

Droppings The waste that comes out of a bird's body when it has digested food.

Fledge	To grow a full set of feathers.
Flock	A group of parakeets.
Fluorescent	Bright and glowing under a certain type of light.
Husks	The tough outer cases of seeds.
Irises	The colored parts of the eyes. In adult parakeets they are light gray.
Mate	Either of a breeding pair.
Molting	When old feathers fall out as new ones grow to replace them.
Nomadic	Traveling from one place to another, without a fixed home.
Nontoxic	Not poisonous.
Plumage	A bird's feathers.
Predators	Animals that hunt other animals.
Preen	To keep feathers clean and neat. Birds preen by taking oil from a gland near their tail and stroking it through their feathers.
Vent	The opening in a bird's backside, where the waste comes out.

Find Out More

Books

Jeffrey, L. S. *Birds: How to Choose and Care for a Bird.* American Humane Pet Care Library. Berkeley Heights, New Jersey: Enslow Publishers, Inc., 2004.

Phillips, M. *Bird World.* Pet's Point of View. Mankato, Minnesota: Compass Point Books, 2004.

Web sites

Budgerigar, Parakeets
animal-world.com/encyclo/birds/parakeets/budgies.php
Plenty of information about budgerigars.

Nature Notes—Budgerigar
www.alicespringsdesertpark.com.au/kids/nature/birds/budgerigar.shtml
Information about wild budgerigars.

Index